Magnets

Catherine Stephens

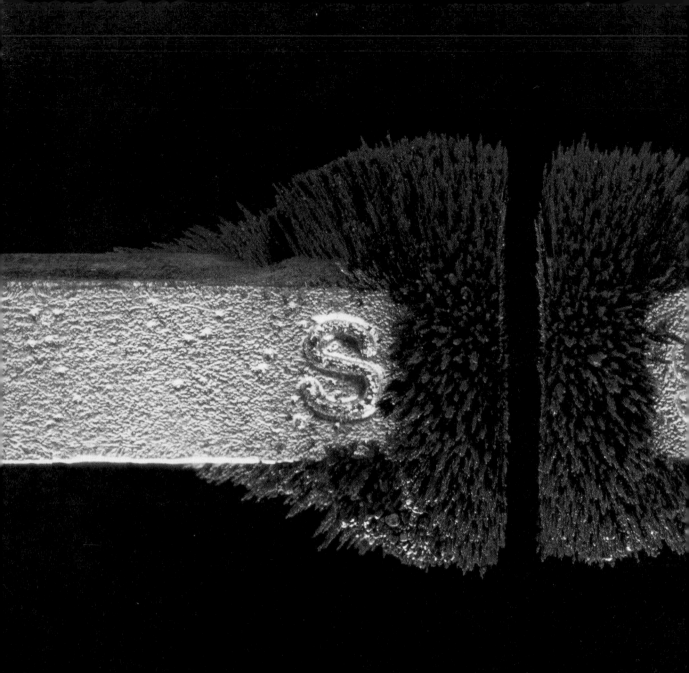

PICTURE CREDITS

Cover, pages 2-3, 4-5 (top, bottom), 9 (top right, center left, bottom left, bottom right), 10, 25 (top right), 26 (bottom right), 31 (top left), 35 (center), Photodisc Green/Getty Images; page 1, Stone/Getty Images; page 5 (top), FirstLight/Picture Quest; page 5 (bottom), David Graham; pages 6-7, Guy Grenier/Masterfile www.masterfile.com; pages 9 (top left), 31 (top right), The Image Bank/Getty Images; page 9 (center right), Photodisc Blue/Getty Images; pages 13 (left), 25 (bottom left), 34 (top), photolibrary.com/Index Stock Imagery, Inc.; page 15, Chase Swift/Corbis; pages 16-17, 18-23 (top border), Gerard Soury/Photo Researchers, Inc.; page 18, Martin Harvey/Corbis; pages 19, 34 (center), Lynda Richardson/ Corbis; pages 18-23 (bottom border), Image Source/Getty Images; page 20 (bottom left), Digital Vision/Getty Images; page 21 (center left), Ron and Valerie Taylor/ www.bciusa.com; page 22 (center left), Nick Caloyiansis/National Geographic Image Collection; pages 22-23 (center), 23 (top right), Associated Press, AP; page 26 (top), Pixland/Index Stock Imagery, Inc.; page 27, Roger Ressmeyer/Corbis; page 28, Ken Lucas/Visuals Unlimited; page 29, Associated Press, Xinhua; page 30 (top left), Richard T. Nowitz/Corbis; page 30 (top right), Mika/zefa/Corbis; page 30 (bottom right), R. Ian Lloyd/Masterfile www.masterfile.com; page 31 (center left), Erich Schrempp/Photo Researchers, Inc.; page 31 (center right), Garry Black/ Masterfile www.masterfile.com; page 31 (bottom left), Creatas/PictureQuest; page 31 (bottom right), Virgo/zefa/Corbis; page 32, Andrew Lambert Photography/Photo Researchers, Inc.; page 33 (top right), Royalty-Free Corbis; page 36, Brandon Cole/Visuals Unlimited.

Produced through the worldwide resources of the National Geographic Society, John M. Fahey, Jr., President and Chief Executive Officer; Gilbert M. Grosvenor, Chairman of the Board; Nina D. Hoffman, Executive Vice President and President, Books and Education Publishing Group.

PREPARED BY NATIONAL GEOGRAPHIC SCHOOL PUBLISHING

Ericka Markman, Senior Vice President and President, Children's Books and Education Publishing Group; Steve Mico, Senior Vice President, Editorial Director, Publisher; Francis Downey, Executive Editor; Richard Easby, Editorial Manager; Bea Jackson, Director of Layout and Design; Jim Hiscott, Design Manager; Cynthia Olson, Art Director; Margaret Sidlosky, Illustrations Director; Matt Wascavage, Manager of Publishing Services; Sean Philpotts, Production Manager; Ted Tucker, Production Specialist.

MANUFACTURING AND QUALITY CONTROL

Christopher A. Liedel, Chief Financial Officer; Phillip L. Schlosser, Director; Clifton M. Brown III, Manager

CONSULTANT AND REVIEWER

Jordan D. Marché II, Ph.D., University of Wisconsin–Madison

BOOK DEVELOPMENT

Amy Sarver

◀ These two magnets have a force that pulls on tiny bits of metal.

Contents

BOOK DESIGN/PHOTO RESEARCH
3R1 Group, Inc.

Copyright © 2006 National Geographic Society.
All Rights Reserved. Reproduction of the whole or any part of the
contents without written permission from the publisher is prohibited.
National Geographic, National Geographic School Publishing,
National Geographic Reading Expeditions, and the Yellow Border
are registered trademarks of the National Geographic Society.

Published by the National Geographic Society
1145 17th Street N.W.
Washington, D.C. 20036-4688

ISBN: 0-7922-5440-6

2010 2009 2008 2007 2006
1 2 3 4 5 6 7 8 9 10 11 12 13 14 15

Printed in Canada.

The Force of Magnets

What is special about a magnet? A magnet is an object that can pull or push things. A magnet pulls or pushes with a force called **magnetism.** You cannot see this force. But you can see how a magnet pulls or pushes things. People use magnets in many ways.

Look at the pictures.

- What magnets do you see?
- How do people use magnets?

....

magnetism – the pulling or pushing force of a magnet

▲ **This magnet holds paper clips.**

4

▲ This magnet pulls coins.

magnets

▲ These magnets hold papers onto a refrigerator.

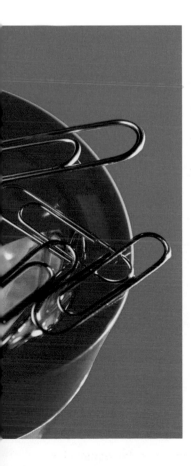

▲ This car magnet is shaped like a soccer ball.

Big Idea
Magnetism is the pulling or pushing force of a magnet.

Set Purpose
Learn about the force of magnets.

Questions You Will Explore

How do magnets work?

What is a magnetic field?

Amaz
M

What pulls these pins to the magnet? The magnet's force **attracts,** or pulls, these objects.

In this book, you will learn about magnets and magnetism. You will discover how magnets work.

....

attract – to pull toward

ing

agnets

Magnetic Fields

All magnets have a **magnetic field.** The magnetic field is the space around a magnet in which the magnet can attract objects.

Suppose you hold a paper clip near a magnet. The magnet attracts the clip. The clip is inside the magnet's magnetic field. What if you move the paper clip farther away? The magnet does not attract the paper clip. The clip is outside the magnet's magnetic field.

magnetic field – the space around a magnet in which the magnet can attract objects

▼ **The paper clip is inside the magnetic field.**   ▼ **The paper clip is outside the magnetic field.**

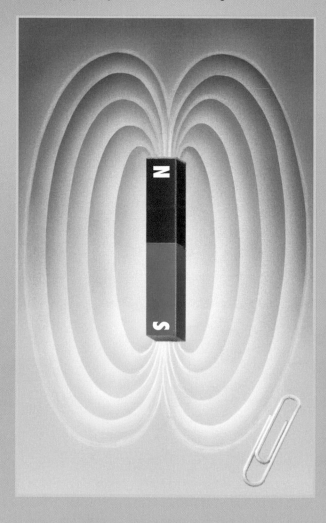

Magnets and Metals

Magnets attract metal objects that are made of iron or steel. Magnets can also attract some other kinds of metals.

A magnet will attract nails. It will also attract silverware and a key. These are all made of iron or steel. A magnet will not attract a plastic ball, a piece of wood, or paper. These objects do not contain iron or steel.

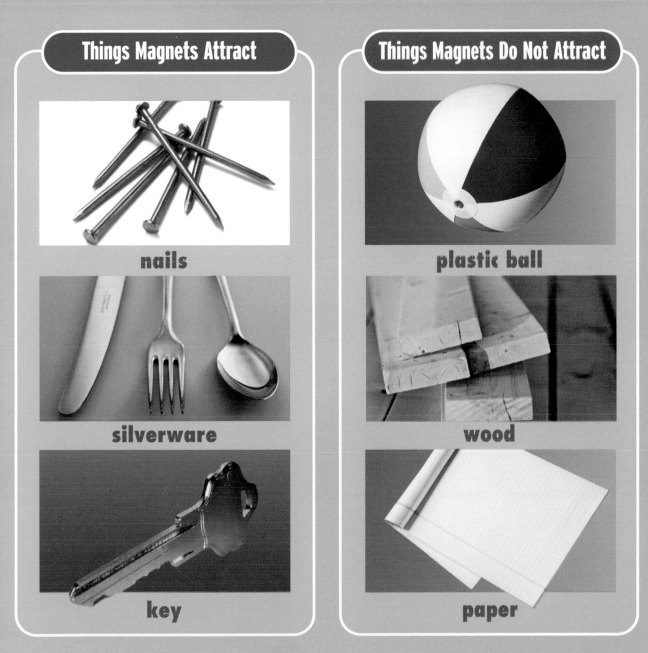

Things Magnets Attract

nails

silverware

key

Things Magnets Do Not Attract

plastic ball

wood

paper

A Pair of Poles

All magnets have two **poles.** The pull of a magnet is strongest at the poles. One pole is called the north pole. The other is the south pole. On the magnet in the picture, the north pole is at one end. The south pole is at the other end.

pole – the area of a magnet where its magnetic field is the strongest

▼ This magnet's north pole (N) and south pole (S) attract little pieces of iron, called iron filings.

north pole

south pole

Poles Pull and Push

The pole of one magnet can pull or push the pole of another magnet. How? The north pole of one magnet will attract the south pole of another magnet.

The pole of one magnet can also **repel,** or push away, the pole of another magnet. Suppose you put the north pole of a magnet near the north pole of another magnet. The magnets will repel each other. The south poles of two magnets will also repel each other.

....

repel – to push away

▼ **Opposite poles attract each other.**

▼ **Like poles repel each other.**

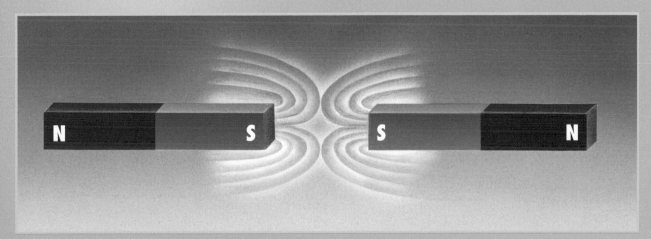

Strong and Weak Magnets

Some magnets are stronger than others. Strong magnets have strong magnetic fields. They can attract objects from far away.

Weaker magnets have weak magnetic fields. They can only attract objects that are close.

▼ A strong magnet has a strong magnetic field.

▼ A weak magnet has a weak magnetic field.

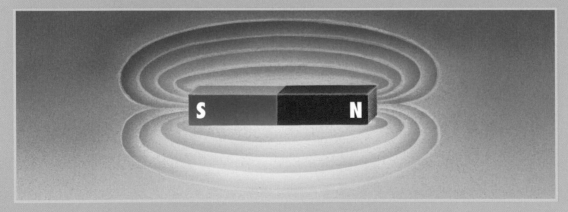

Many Sizes and Shapes

Magnets come in many sizes and shapes. In school, you might use a magnet shaped like a horseshoe. There are round and bar-shaped magnets, too. Most magnets used in our homes or schools are small. Their magnetic fields are weak.

Look at the huge magnet in the picture below. This magnet lifts iron and steel parts from a car junkyard. It has a strong magnetic field.

▼ This large magnet has a strong magnetic field. It can lift large pieces of iron and steel.

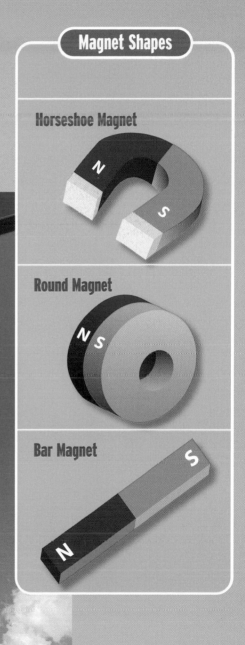

Magnet Shapes

Horseshoe Magnet

Round Magnet

Bar Magnet

Earth Is a Magnet

Large magnets are not just in junkyards. Earth itself is a magnet! Earth has a magnetic north pole. Earth also has a magnetic south pole. Like all magnets, Earth has a magnetic field around it. You cannot see Earth's magnetic field. But it is all around you.

▼ Earth is a large magnet.

magnetic north pole

magnetic south pole

Magnetism on Earth

Earth's magnetic field is important. Many living things depend on it. How? Some animals travel long distances during their lives. Some scientists think Earth's magnetic field guides these animals as they travel.

There are many ways that magnetism is important in our world. Magnets can hold things together. They can push things apart. Magnets give us an amazing force that we use each day.

Stop and Think!

HOW are all magnets alike?

▼ Earth's magnetic field may guide geese as they fly long distances.

Recap
Explain how Earth is like other magnets.

Set Purpose
Learn how Earth's magnetism is important to sea turtles.

▼ A loggerhead turtle swims through the ocean.

Magne
Sea Tu

During its life, a loggerhead turtle swims thousands of miles. Loggerheads follow the same path across the ocean. How do they know where to go? Earth's magnetic field may help the turtles find their way.

tism and
rtles

Into the Ocean

From the start, loggerhead turtles seem to know where to go. They begin life as eggs. The eggs hatch. The small turtles find themselves on a sandy beach in Florida. Right away, the turtles race to the ocean.

Once in the water, the turtles start swimming. They swim in the same direction. They follow the same path around the Atlantic Ocean. Their parents are not around to show them the way. How do they know where to go?

▲ As soon as the turtles hatch, they race to the ocean.

▲ A baby loggerhead
swims in the ocean.

Using Earth's Magnetism

Some scientists think that loggerheads use Earth's
magnetic field to guide them. As a turtle swims,
it can feel changes in Earth's magnetic field.
These changes tell the turtle that it is time to
swim in a different direction. Let's take a look at
how a loggerhead turtle makes its **journey.**

....

journey – a long trip

Heading East

A loggerhead's journey begins in the ocean near Florida. The turtles feel the pull from Earth's magnetic field. This causes the turtles to turn east. They then swim across the Atlantic Ocean.

United States

Florida

1

Magnetism causes the turtle to swim east across the Atlantic Ocean.

Path of Loggerhead Turtles

North

West East

South

Atlantic Ocean

2 The turtle feels a change in Earth's magnetic field and turns south.

3 The turtle turns northwest and heads back to Florida where its journey began.

Changing Directions

The turtle swims for months across the ocean. What happens when it gets to the other side? It feels another change in Earth's magnetic field. This causes the turtle to turn south. After swimming south, the loggerhead makes a final turn. The turtle swims back to Florida. That is where its long journey began.

A Long Journey

It takes five to ten years for a loggerhead to complete its journey. It swims more than 12,900 kilometers (8,000 miles). The path that a loggerhead takes helps the turtle stay alive. The ocean water along its path is warm. There is plenty of food. Outside the turtle's path, the water is colder. Food is harder to find.

▲ Turtles that follow Earth's magnetic field find plenty of food.

▲ Scientists carry a loggerhead turtle that they are studying.

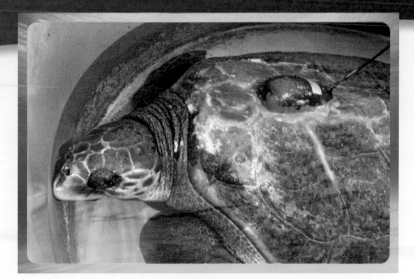

▲ This loggerhead turtle has a radio on its back. The radio lets scientists follow the turtle on its journey.

Studying Loggerheads

Do loggerheads feel magnetic fields? Scientists test this idea with experiments. They create a magnetic field near loggerheads. This magnetic field makes the turtles swim in a new direction. Scientists also put radios on the backs of loggerheads. This lets scientists follow the loggerheads as they swim through the ocean.

There is still a lot to learn. But some scientists believe that loggerheads use Earth's magnetic field to find their way.

Stop and Think!

HOW is magnetism important to loggerhead sea turtles?

Recap
Explain how magnetism is important to sea turtles.

Set Purpose
Read these articles to learn more about magnetism.

CONNECT WHAT YOU HAVE LEARNED

Magnets and Magnetism

Magnetism is all around you. Even Earth has a magnetic field. Magnets can attract or repel some kinds of metals.

Here are some ideas you learned about magnetism.

- All magnets have a magnetic field.
- Magnets have a north pole and south pole.
- Some magnets have a stronger magnetic field than other magnets.
- Earth is a large magnet.

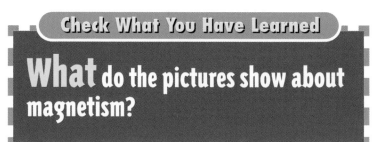

Check What You Have Learned

What do the pictures show about magnetism?

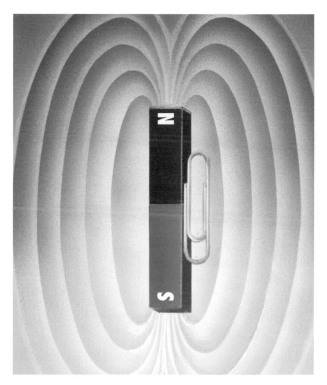

▲ A magnet has a magnetic field.

▲ A magnet's pull is strongest at its north pole and south pole.

▲ This magnet has a strong magnetic field.

▲ Earth is a magnet with a large magnetic field.

map

compass

▲ These hikers use a compass and map to find their way.

The Point of a Compass

Look at this compass. You see a needle inside. A compass needle is a magnet. It is pulled by Earth's magnetic field. A compass needle points toward Earth's magnetic north pole. This helps people find their way when they travel.

needle

Many people use compasses. Hikers use maps and compasses to help them find their way on land. Sailors use maps, charts, and compasses to find their way on the ocean.

▲ The needle of the compass points to Earth's magnetic north pole.

Space Boots

Astronauts are scientists who travel into space. Life in space is not easy. Things inside the spacecraft float in the air. Pencils, paper, and even people float if there is not something to hold them to the spacecraft. This makes walking very hard.

So scientists made special walking boots for astronauts. The boots had magnets inside. The magnets in the boots were attracted to the metal floor of the spacecraft. This allowed the astronauts to walk inside the spacecraft.

▶ **This astronaut wears space boots that help him walk in space.**

astronaut

space boots

Maglev Trains

Most trains have an engine in front that pulls the other train cars along a track. But there is no engine pulling this maglev train. Magnets make it move. There are strong magnets on the bottom of a maglev train. The track has magnets, too. The magnets on the train and track attract and repel each other to move the train.

| **maglev** | **mag** - comes from the word *magnetic* |
| | **lev** - comes from the word *levitate*, which means to rise into the air |

CONNECT TO ROCKS

▲ **Magnetite attracts these metal paper clips.**

28

▲ The world's fastest maglev train is this one in China.

Magnetic Rocks

Long ago, people found some strange rocks. According to one story, the iron nails in a man's shoe stuck to these rocks. People called them magic rocks.

Today, we call these rocks lodestones. A lodestone acts like a magnet. That is because lodestones contain a lot of magnetite. Magnetite is a mineral that is magnetic.

Many kinds of words are used in this book. Here you will learn about synonyms. You will also learn about multiple-meaning words.

Synonyms

Synonyms are words that have the same meaning. Find the synonyms below. Then use each synonym in a new sentence.

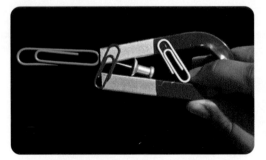

A magnet **attracts** these paper clips.

The girl **pulls** the rope.

One magnet's south pole **repels** the other magnet's south pole.

The boy **pushes** the boat.

Multiple-Meaning Words

A multiple-meaning word is a word that has more than one meaning. Find the multiple-meaning words below. Then use each multiple-meaning word in a new sentence.

The **point** on the compass shows the direction north.

People **point** to the sky.

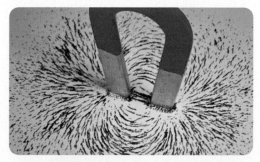

All magnets have a magnetic **field.**

Grass grows in the **field.**

A magnet attracts the **iron** nails.

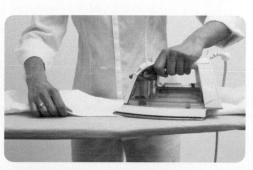

An **iron** takes wrinkles out of clothes.

Write About Magnetism

Research what objects are attracted to a magnet. Then write a summary telling what you learned.

Research

Walk around your classroom and touch different objects with a magnet.

Take Notes

List the names of the objects you touch with the magnet. Tell whether or not each object is attracted to the magnet.

Write

Write a summary that explains your research. Tell which objects were attracted to your magnet and which ones were not. Describe ways that the objects attracted to the magnet are alike.

Read and Compare

Read More About Magnets

Find and read other books about magnets. As you read, think about these questions.

- What is magnetism?
- What do all magnets have in common?
- Why do scientists study magnetism?

Books to Read

NATIONAL GEOGRAPHIC
READING EXPEDITIONS
PHYSICAL SCIENCE
The Mystery of Magnets
PAMELA BLISS

NATIONAL GEOGRAPHIC
READING EXPEDITIONS
PHYSICAL SCIENCE
Matter, Matter Everywhere
STEPHEN M. TOMECEK

NATIONAL GEOGRAPHIC
READING EXPEDITIONS
PHYSICAL SCIENCE
Using Force and Motion
GLEN PHELAN

▲ Read about magnetism and how it is used.

▲ Read about properties of things on Earth.

▲ Read about forces that move objects.

Glossary

attract (page 7)
To pull toward
Magnets attract iron and steel.

journey (page 19)
A long trip
A loggerhead turtle takes a journey across the
Atlantic Ocean.

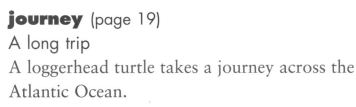

magnetic field (page 8)
The space around a magnet in which the magnet
can attract objects
The paper clip is inside the magnet's magnetic field.

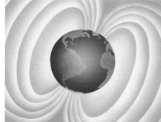

magnetism (page 4)
The pulling or pushing force of a magnet
Earth's magnetism guides some animals as they travel.

pole (page 10)
The area of a magnet where its magnetic field is the strongest
The iron filings are attracted to the poles of this magnet.

repel (page 11)
To push away
The south poles of these magnets repel each other.

Index